THE ANGLO-SAXON SCOP

BY

L. F. ANDERSON, M.A.

FOLCROFT LIBRARY EDITIONS / 1973

Library of Congress Cataloging in Publication Data

Anderson, Lewis Flint, 1866-1932.
    The Anglo-Saxon scop.

    Original ed. issued as no. 1 of University of
Toronto studies. Philological series.
    Originally presented as the author's thesis
(M.A.), University of Toronto, 1902.
    1. Bards and bardism. 2. Anglo-Saxon poetry--
History and criticism. I. Title. II. Series:
Toronto. University. University of Toronto studies.
Philological series, no. 1.
PR203.A5 1973   829'.1   73-1780
ISBN 0-8414-1703-2

THE ANGLO-SAXON SCOP

BY

L. F. ANDERSON, M.A.

PREFATORY NOTE

This study of the Anglo-Saxon Scop was presented to the University of Toronto, as a thesis for the degree of M.A., in 1902. As examiner in the subject I drew the attention of the Editor of the University Studies to the essay and recommended it as one suitable for publication. It was accepted by the Committee and now appears as the first of a philological series, which it is hoped will prove useful to all interested in the subject. The essay is the result of four years' study of Anglo-Saxon in University College, Toronto, followed by post-graduate work with Professors Wülker and Sievers, of Leipzig. The author is now Professor of Pedagogy in the Normal College in Marquette, Michigan.

DAVID R. KEYS,
Associate Professor of Anglo-Saxon,
University College, Toronto.

ANALYSIS.

THE ANGLO-SAXON SCOP.

This essay is an endeavour to contribute something toward greater definiteness in our conception of the professional singer among the Anglo-Saxons, by "Anglo-Saxons" being meant those races whose language and literature are designated Anglo-Saxon. The investigation covers the period extending from the date of the earliest extant Anglo-Saxon poem to the time of the decay of the scop's art, perhaps in the eighth or ninth century.

Sources of Information.

The most direct and the most reliable sources of information are the specimens of Anglo-Saxon poetry which have come down to us from the period above mentioned. The poems *Widsith*, *Beowulf* and *Deor's Complaint* contain nearly all the information obtainable in Anglo-Saxon literature itself concerning the professional singer. Composed throughout a period of possibly one or more centuries they reflect in a blurred, indefinite, composite picture the social conditions of the race through an extended period of time. *Widsith* is for our investigations of the greatest value. It is an account composed originally by a court singer of his experiences in the practice of his profession. It bears the marks of being of greater age than the other two poems. In its earliest form it described a journey to the court of the Gothic king Eormanric. Hence it dates probably from the fourth century. The epic *Beowulf* affords us in different passages an insight into the rude court life which was the scene of the scop's professional activity. In it we see the scop in the performance of his professional duties. The poem itself is an aggregation of several interesting specimens of the scop's art. In its earliest form it was composed probably in the early part of the seventh century.[1] *Deor's Complaint* is a lyrical poem composed by a singer concerning himself. It furnishes one or

---

[1] Wülker, *Grundriss*, p. 306.

[5]

two interesting details regarding the life of the Anglo-Saxon scop, and indicates his familiarity with the great body of the Germanic sagas.

In the rest of Anglo-Saxon literature references to the professional singer are comparatively rare. The fragments *The Fight at Finnsburg* and *Waldere* are silent on the subject, and in the later heroic poems of the Christian period, *Byrhtnoth's Death* and the chronicle poems, the poet stands entirely in the background. In the brief reference which Cynewulf makes to his own career in *The Finding of the Cross*, we have an interesting picture of the poet nature freeing itself from the traditions of the scop and adapting itself to the new order of things under the sway of Christianity. One of the riddles usually attributed to him has for its subject the travelling singer. The information afforded by occasional passages in other Anglo-Saxon poems is relatively unimportant. The Anglo-Saxon laws and the works of William of Malmesbury and Ingulf, together with the Saxon Chronicle, give us some insight into the life of the professional singer of the eighth, ninth and tenth centuries.

The specimens of scop poetry which have been preserved to us date from a period when the Anglo-Saxons were inhabiting the mainland of Europe. On certain points concerning which the evidence afforded by Anglo-Saxon sources has been uncertain or altogether wanting, reference will be made to the laws and literature of the other Germanic races of the continent. The social conditions amid which the Anglo-Saxon scop flourished seem to be reproduced in many important respects among the Scandinavians three or four centuries later. For this reason a comparison of the facts we possess regarding the professional singers of the two peoples is instructive.

Origin and Development of the Scop's Profession.

No authoritative information is attainable as to the period at which the poet-singers became in a sense professional. Among the Finns, who in recent years possess a folk poetry and folk customs presenting many analogies with those of the Germanic society of our period, the professional singer has not yet made his appearance. "Trotz dieser dichterischen Anlage und dem Bewusstsein derselben, haben die Sänger bei den Finnen doch niemals eine besondere Zunft gebildet, noch war das Dichten und Singen ein Beruf" (Comparetti, *Kalevala*, German translation, p. 19).

Gautier (*Les Épopées françaises*, ii. p. 4) supposes with some plausibility that the singers assumed a more and more professional character along with the development of the epic. " Tant que la poésie primitive conserve le caractère lyrique, le peuple tout entier sait par cœur ses poèmes et les chante lui-même ; mais dès que les louanges des héros se changent en une narration plus étendue, il devient nécessaire que certaines mémoires professionelles se chargent de narrer ces exploits, comme aussi certaines voix de les chanter. Bref, l'heure de l'épopée a sonné, et pour répandre et populariser cette épopée qui se chante, il faut des chanteurs de profession, il faut des hommes du métier."

The composition and recitation or singing of poetry seem to have been common accomplishments among all the early Anglo-Saxons, indeed among all the early Germanic tribes. The king Hrothgar in *Beowulf* takes the harp and sings. King Gunnar of the Norse legend was so skilled in music that he could play with his toes. From Bæda's account of Cædmon we learn that simple farm labourers were accustomed at their meetings to compose and sing in turn, acccmpanying themselves with the harp. Yet it seems very evident that certain singers endowed with unusual talent adopted the art as a profession. Of the professional singers definitely mentioned in Anglo-Saxon literature, two, Deor and Hrothgar's scop, are especially spoken of as attached in that capacity to the court of a chief or king, and the scop of *Widsith* in all likelihood occupies a similar position. It is surprising that the small body of Anglo-Saxon literature preserved to us should contain such clear evidence of this fact. It is doubtful if a like amount of modern poetry would afford an equally definite idea of the standing of the modern poet.

Professional Singers among Germanic Tribes other than Anglo-Saxon.

Tacitus,* our earliest authority in the history of Germanic

---

*Ann. i, 65 ; Hist. v, 15.

poetry, makes no mention of a professional poet-singer, but it is reasonable to suppose that the choric songs he refers to were rendered under professional or semi-professional leadership. Jordanes states that the Eastern Goths were accustomed in the fifth century to songs celebrating the deeds of their national heroes, which were sung to the accompaniment of the harp. "Ante quos etiam cantu majorum facta modulationibus citharisque canebant, Eterpamara, Hanale, Fridigerni, Vidigoiæ et aliorum, quorum in hac gente magna opinio est, quales vix heroas fuisse miranda jactat antiquitas" (*De Orig. Actibusque Get.*, c. 5). Perhaps the earliest definite reference to professional singers is given by Priscus in his account of a feast celebrated by Attila in *the manner of the Goths.* When evening came on torches were lighted and two singers stood before the king and recited songs that had been composed concerning his victories and his warlike virtues. "Ἐπιγενομένης δὲ ἑσπέρας δᾷδες ἀνήφθησαν, δύο δὲ ἀντικρὺ τοῦ Ἀττήλα παρελθόντες βάρβαροι ἄσματα πεποιημένα ἔλεγον, νίκας αὐτοῦ καὶ τὰς κατὰ πόλεμον ᾄδοντες ἀρετάς" (*Hist. Goth.*, p. 205. Bonn, 1829).

Not only were the Goths among the first of the Germanic tribes to cultivate epic poetry, but they cultivated it with such success that many of their heroic songs were adopted by kindred races and were preserved after their own native poetry was forgotten. On this point Kögel in his recent history of German literature says: "Dafür spricht der Umstand, dass gerade die bedeutendsten und beliebtesten Sagenstoffe gotischen Ursprungs sind: Ermanrich, die Harlunge, Dietrich v. Bern, Heime, Witig, Hildebrand und Hadubrand, wahrscheinlich auch Walther v. Aquitanien, sind gotische Helden, und die Nibelungensage ist, von dem frankischen Sigfridsmythus abgesehen, eine dichterische That der Burgunden, die mit den Gothen auf das nächste verwandt sind" (*Geschichte der deutschen Litteratur*, I, i, 134).

That their influence extended to the Saxons is proven by the fact that the Anglo-Saxon poem *Widsith* contains an extract from a Gothic epic, as well as by the fact that frequent mention is made of Gothic heroes in Anglo-Saxon literature. But they exerted the most powerful influence upon the Langobards, a neighbouring race. The epic poetry of this people has succumbed to the powerful Romanizing influences to which they were subjected, but the prose digest of it given by Paulus Diaconus and Origo show that it was of great richness and extent. These songs were known among professional singers of several other Germanic tribes. Alboin, one of the great heroes of the Langobard historic epics, is mentioned in *Widsith*. Paulus Diaconus states himself that the fame of Alboin was carried far and wide in songs even to the Bavarians and the Saxons. "Alboin vero ita praeclarum longe lateque nomen percrebuit ut hactenus etiam tam apud Baioariorum gentem quamque et Saxonum, sed et alios eiusdem linguae homines eius liberalitas et gloria bellorumque felicitas et virtus in eorum carminibus celebretur" (Paulus Diaconus, I, 27). Kögel (*op. cit.* I, i, 122) states that this extension of Alboin's fame was the work of the professional singer: "In diesen Liedern, die durch die von Hof zu Hofe ziehenden Berufssänger verbreitet wurden, waren also Alboins grosse Eigenschaften und Ehren gepriesen."

About the year 500 Chlodowech, the founder of the Frankish kingdom, applied to Theodoric the Great for a harper, *citharœdus*: "Cum rex Francorum convivi nostri fama pellectus a nobis citharœdum magnis precibus expetisset" (Cassiodorus, *Var.* II, 40). "Citharœdum arte sua doctum destinavimus expetitum, qui ore manibusque consona voce cantando gloriam vestræ potestatis oblectet" (*Ib.*, II, 41). It is not absolutely certain whether by this name we are to understand the Gothic professional poet-singer or the entertainer of the Romanic races, the prototype of the jongleurs of France. Kögel adopts the former view: "Mit der Uebersiedelung des gotischen Sängers an den frankischen Hof trat ein Wendepunkt des poetischen Geschmacks ein: nunmehr wird das unstrophische, von Kunstdichtern gepflegte epische Heldenlied bei den Franken und wohl auch bei allen anderen Westgermanen etwa mit Ausnahme der Langobarden eingeführt, dass die einheimischen Ansätze bald ganz zurückdrängt" (*Op. cit.* I, i, 130).

Two passages in Venantius Fortunatus prove that the Germanic professional singer was known among the Franks of the eighth century. In Carmen VII, 8 the poet addresses Duke Lupus of Aquitania—

"Romanusque lyra, plaudat tibi barbarus harpa" (v. 65).

*   *   *   *   *   *   *

" Nos tibi versiculos, dent barbara carmina leudos :
sic variante tropo laus sonet una viro " (v. 69).

Again in the *Praefatio* to his poems the poet refers to the
songs sung during the progress of the meal : " Ubi me tantun-
dem valebat raucum .gemere quod cantare apud quos nihil
disparat aut stridor anseris aut canor oloris, sola sæpe bombi-
cans barbaros leudos harpa relidens " (*Monum. Germ. Hist. :
Auct.* IV, 2, l. 12).

A passage in Carmen XII of Apollinaris Sidonius indicates
that professional singers were known among the Burgundians
of the fifth century—

> " Quid me, etsi valeam, parare carmen
> Fescenninicolae iubes Diones
> inter crinigeras situm catervas
> . et Germanica verba sustinentem,
> laudantem tetrico subinde vultu
> quod Burgundio cantat esculentus
> infundens acido comam butyro?
> vis dicam tibi quid poema frangat ?
> ex hoc barbaricis abacta plectris
> spernit senipedem stilum Thalia
> ex quo septipedes videt patronos."   (v. 1-11.)

That professional singers were known among the Frisians of
the eighth century is proven by a passage in Altfrid's life of St.
Liudger : "Illo discumbente cum discipulis suis, oblatus est
caecus vocabulo Berulef qui a vicinis suis valde diligebatur, eo
quod esset affabilis et antiquorum actus regumque certamina
bene noverat psallendo promere " (Pertz, *Monumenta : Scrip-
tores,* II, 412). In commenting on the expression " regum
certamina," Mone, in his work *Niederländ. Volkslitteratur* (p.
373), states his belief that we have in the above passage a reference to Germanic folk-poetry. If he is not mistaken we have
in Berulef a representative of the professional or semi-professional singers directly or indirectly referred to in the passages
which I quote. " Nun hatten die Frisen keine Könige, obgleich
Rathbot mehrmals König genannt wird, die Lieder bezogen sich
daher wahrscheinlich auf ältere Ereignisse teutscher Völker

überhaupt, woran die Frisen entweder durch Handlungen oder nur durch die Sage Antheil hatten." That it was the custom among the Frisians to celebrate the deeds of their forefathers in song is expressly stated in another version of the same incident quoted by the brothers Grimm in *Deutsche Sagen* (vol. 2, p. xi) from an old Cassel manuscript : " Is, Berulef cognomento, vicinis suis admodum carus erat, quia antiquorum actus regumque certamina, more gentis suae, non inurbane cantare noverat." The professional singers among the Frisians were so numerous and so highly esteemed that they were placed under the special protection of the law : " Qui harpatorem, qui cum circulo harpare potest, in manum percusserit, componat illud quarta parte majore compositione quam alteri ejusdem conditionis homini : aurifici similiter : foeminae fresum facienti similiter " (Pertz, *Monumenta : Leges*, III, 699 : *Lex Frisionum*).

Poetry and Music among the Anglo-Saxons.

The Angles, to whom we are indebted for the earlier Anglo-Saxon poetry, seem in their national character to have been peculiarly adapted to the production of a great national literature. Their character is thus sketched by Freytag :— " Zuerst die Angeln von der nordalbingischen Halbinsel. Dort war vom 4ten bis 6ten Jahrhundert vielleicht höheres Gedeihen und grössere Cultur als bei einem anderen Volk zwischen Oder und Rhein. Seefahrt und unablässige Verbindung mit der Fremde, Beutezüge und Handel hatten den Angeln reichen Goldschatz zugeführt, ihre Runen und geschlagenen Schmuckstücke, ihre Heldensagen und die Colonization der nordenglischen Landschaften welche sie in dieser Zeit ausführen, lassen erkennen wie tüchtig die Kraft war, welche wir von deutschem Boden fast ganz verloren haben. Dass sie ein gescheutes, gedankenvolles Volk waren, von einer rührenden Innigkeit der Empfindung, lehrt die edle germanische Poesie der Angelsachsen in den nächsten Jahrhunderten : den Angeln möchte man aus dieser Poesie die sinnvolle Betrachtung des Lebens, grössere Zartheit und höheren Gedankenflug zueignen als den kernhaften Sachsen " (*Bilder aus der deutschen Vergangenheit*, I, 134).

Numerous allusions in the historic records of the Anglo-Saxons lead us to believe that they were distinguished even among the Germanic peoples by their love of poetry and song. The Cædmon incident shows how common among them was the custom of singing and reciting poetry in the 7th century. Aldhelm (Faricii, c. 1110, *Vita S. Aldhelmi*) wins from the Anglo-Saxons a hearing for the teachings of Christianity by appearing as a singer and reciter. Certain facts from the later history of the Anglo-Saxons afford us evidence of a similar kind. A passage from the life of Dunstan shows that he learned the songs sung by the people and could play on the harp. "Hic etiam inter sacra litterarum studia, ut in omnibus esset idoneus, artem scribendi nec non citharizandi pariterque pingendi peritiam diligenter excoluit. Sumpsit secum ex more citharam suam, quam lingua paterna hearpam vocamus" (*Vita S. Dunstan*, Bericht d. Akad. zu Wien, xiii, 150). Alfred in his boyhood received as a prize an illuminated manuscript of Anglo-Saxon poems. As a man he entered the Danish camp in the guise of a harper. Asser states that the princes Edward and Aelthrythe studied Saxon books, chiefly Saxon poems. Many of the songs current in the late Saxon period were of an historical character. Malmesbury acknowledges his indebtedness to the songs of his day for certain historic facts and he later refers to incidents as having already become, through songs, matters of common knowledge (Turner, *History of the Anglo-Saxons*, III, pp. 52, 56). Vogt in his *Leben und Dichten der deutschen Spielleute* states that the professional singer of the Germanic races first makes his appearance in history among the Anglo-Saxons : "Sänger von Gewerbe treten für uns zuerst nicht auf deutschem Boden, sondern bei einem Stamme auf, der, vom Grundstock der germanischen Nation losgelöst, doch noch auf lange Zeit den scharf ausgeprägten germanischen Character bewahrte, bei den Angelsachsen" (p. 4).

The most direct and the most reliable evidence we have of the fondness of the Anglo-Saxons for poetry, music and song is found in their literature itself. "Nis hearpan wyn, gomen gleobeames" sings the poet in *Beowulf* (1.2263) in painting a scene of gloom and desolation. Farther on in the same poem,

in emphasizing the dreariness of a deserted abode, the hero
Beowulf is represented as saying,

"nis þaer hearpan sweg
        gomen in geardum, swylce þaer iu waeron" (1:2459).

On this passage Köhler in *Germania* XV remarks, "Als
bedeutsam ist hervorzuheben der Gedanke am Schlusse der
Rede jenes alten Heiden, der sich zu seinen Schätzen in die
Felsenhöhle verbirgt, und sich zum Lindwurm verwandelt, dass
nun die Wonne der Harfe, die Lust des Saitenspiels zu Ende
sei." The Seafarer in the poem of that name pictures vividly
the desperate condition of the storm-tossed mariner when he
says (l.44),

"Ne biþ him to hearpan hyge."

Likewise the Wanderer in his exile,

"no þær fela bringeþ
        cuþra cwidegiedda" (*Wanderer*, l.54).

In the "Lament of the Fallen Angels" the latter remind themselves of the happiness they formerly enjoyed in heaven in the
following terms,

"Þær habbaþ englas
    eadigne dream sanctas singaþ." (Grein, II, 2, ll. 354-355.)

Song had been one of their chief delights in heaven, and the
remembrance of it adds to their present misery :

"Is me nu wyrsæ þæt ic wuldres leoht
        uppe mid englum æfre cuþe,
        song on swegle, þær sunu meotodes
        habbaþ eadigne bearn ealle ymbfangen
        seolfa mid sange" (*Ib.* ll. 141-145).

Even the vocabulary of the Anglo-Saxons indicates the high
esteem in which they held the arts of poetry and song. On
this point I cannot do better than quote from Stosch, *Hofdienst
der Spielleute*, p. 6 : "Die bilderreiche Sprache der Angelsachsen nannte Lied und Spiel 'Freude' (gleo), 'Wonne' (wynn),
'Jubel' (dream) ; den Gesang 'die Lust der Halle' (healgamen),
und die Harfe 'das Lustholz' (gamenwudu), 'den Freudenbaum'
(gleobeam). Derselbe Ehrentitel zierte den Spielmann, wenn er
'gleoman' (Freudenmann) und seine Kunst 'gleocraft' (die
röhliche Kunst) hiess." Music and song represent joy and glad-

ness.   In the joyous feasts held in Heorot, previous to its inva-
sion by the monster Grendel, "þær wæs hearpan sweg swutol
sang scopes" (*Beowulf*, 89-90).   Not until Beowulf had rid
the Danes of this terror are song and music again mentioned.
In the rejoicings over Beowulf's victory,

> "hwilum cyninges þegn
> guma gilphlæden, gidda gemyndig,
> se þe ealfela ealdgesegena
> worn gemunde, word oþer fand
> soþe gebunden" (*Beowulf*, 867).

Hrothgar's scop busies himself with the composition of a poem
celebrating Beowulf's exploit :

> "secg eft ongan
> siþ Beowulfes snyttrum styrian" (*Beow.*, 871-872).

The author of the poetical paraphrase of Genesis lingers fondly
over the brief reference to music given in that book.

> "Jubal noma se þurh gleawne geþanc
> herbuendra hearpan ærest
> handum sinum hlyn awehte
> swinsigende sweg sunu Lamechs" (*Genesis*, 1078-81).

We have no evidence that the Anglo-Saxon poet-singers, or
indeed the singers of any Germanic tribe of our period, possessed among themselves any sort of organization.   The numerous references quoted elsewhere make it evident, however, that
certain members of the Anglo-Saxon, and of the other early
Germanic tribes, practised the art of the poet-singer as a profession.   On this point, Weinhold, in his work entitled *Deutsche
Frauen* (II, 130), writes : "Ueberdies waren unter den Germanen
seit alter Zeit, wenn auch keine Sängerkaste, so doch Sänger
und Spielleute vorhanden, welche die Kunst zur Lebensberuf
gemacht hatten."   Although some of the scops mentioned were
presumably of noble birth, Widsith for instance, there is nothing
to show that they were drawn from any particular class of
society.

The Scop's Sphere of Activity.

Anglo-Saxon literature affords us glimpses into different
phases of the life of the singer.   We see him occupying a
definite position in the household of a chief or a king as do Deor

and Heorrenda in the "Singer's Complaint" and Hrothgar's scop in *Beowulf;* we find him again travelling about from court to court as did Widsith, or, in a much later period, wandering here and there seeking patrons among all classes of society as did the younger Cynewulf and the singer of the riddle. "Der Sänger hiess Scop und entweder war er bei einem Könige oder Edeling in festem Dienst, oder zog mit seiner Kunst, wie einer jener holsteinischen Sänger, an fremden Höfen umher, stets Lohn empfangend." (Müllenhof, *Sagen, Märchen u. Lieder aus Schleswig-Holstein,* XI.)

The Scop as Court Singer.

The chief duty of the official court-singer among the old Germanic tribes was that of entertaining the chief and his warrior-band with song and story. "Die germanischen Fürsten strebten danach, ihre Hofhaltungen durch Männer zu schmücken, welche den Schatz der alten Sagen und Lieder besassen und deren Geschicklichkeit im Harfenspiel das allgemeine Maass überstieg." (Weinhold, *op. cit.* II, 130.)

The particular occasions which brought the scop into greatest prominence were the feasts in which the ancient Germans took such delight. The entertainment, however, did not devolve entirely upon the scop. Skill in narration and in music, as we learn from *Beowulf* and from Bæda, were not uncommon among Anglo-Saxons of all classes. There were then as now amateur as well as professional poets and singers. The thanes of the hall passed the harp from hand to hand and at times even the king would participate. The chief musical and rhetorical entertainment, however, was afforded by the scop, whose poems were distinguished both as to excellence of form and of delivery from those of the ordinary amateur. Thus in the feasts in Heorot,

"þær wæs hearpan sweg,
swutol sang scopes." (*Beowulf,* 89-90.)

Again at the feast at which Beowulf and his followers were received by Hrothgar,

"scop hwilum sang,
hador on Heorote : þær wæs hæleþa dream,
duguþ unlytel Dena und Wedera." (*Beow.* 496-499.)

At the feast in honour of Beowulf's victory the scop recites the
Finn saga.   The passage in *Beowulf* in which this fact is mentioned seems to indicate in its elaborate and pompous phrase-
ology the importance attached to this part of the entertainment.

> Þær wæs sang and swег samod ætgædere
> fore Healfdenes hildewisan,
> gomenwudu greted, gid oft wrecen,
> þonne healgamen Hroþgares scop
> æfter medobence mænan scolde:
> Finnes eaferum."   (*Beow.* 1065 *et seq.*)

In honour of the same event the Sigemund saga was also sung.

> " Secg eft ongan
> on sped wrecan spel gerade,
> wordum wrixlan, welhwylc gecweþ
> þæt he fram Sigemunde secgan hyrde.   (*Ib.* 871 *et seq.*)

The scop as a master in the poetic art would have his memory richly stored with mythic and heroic lore.   It is interesting
from a psychological point of view to note how the singer Deor
in his lament compares his lot with those of various heroes
whose fates he had so often sung.   The mind of Widsith seems
so charged with sagas that the mere names of some of the
heroic characters impel him to recite favourite passages from the
sagas in which they figure.   For example,

> " Wudgan and Hamar
> ne wæran þæt gesiþa þa sæmestan,
> þeahþe ic hy anihst nemnan sceolde.
> Fuloft of þam heape hwinende fleag
> giellende gar on grome þeode."   (*Wid.* 124 *et seq.*)

The great number of sagas learned by the scop of *Beowulf* is
expressly mentioned,

> " hwilum cyninges þegn
> guma gilp-hlæden gidda gemyndig,
> se þe eal-fela eald gesegena
> worn gemunde, word oþer fand
> soþe gebunden."   (*Beow.* 868-872.)

It was praiseworthy in a scop to have learned not only the
more familiar sagas, but some not generally known.   Thus of

the singer in *Beowulf* it is said that he recited all that he had heard men say of Sigemund and thereto much hitherto unknown.

" wel-hwylc gecwæþ
Þæt he fram Sigemundes secgan hyrde
ellen-dædum, uncuþes fela. (*Ib.* 875-7.)

The Scops the Conservators of the Knowledge of Their Time.

The scop sang not only sagas but poems in which were embodied the rude science and philosophy of his time. One of the poems by Hrothgar's scop is a sort of rude poetical treatise on cosmogony, a topic which occupies a large place in the literature of the Scandinavians and which seems to have possessed peculiar interest for the northern Germans.

" Þær wæs hearpan sweg,
swutol sang scopes. Sægde, se þe cuþe
frumsceaft fira feorran reccan,
cwæþ, þæt se ælmihtiga eorþan worhte,
wlitebeorhtne wang, swa wæter bebugeþ." (*Ib.* 89 *et seq.*)

The Scop as Teacher.

It is probable that the scop was looked upon as one whose function was not merely to entertain but also to instruct. The sagas which he repeated to the old Germans were to them something far different from what they are to us. They embodied their history and their theology. Hence the transition is easy from the saga to poems more directly didactic such as the one just referred to. Thirst for knowledge and for wisdom was one of the most prominent traits in the character of the Germans of the early centuries of the Christian era. Meyer emphasizes this point in his *Altgermanische Poesie*. On pages 528-529 he writes—" Lernen und Kämpfen fanden wir als Lieblingsideen der alten Germanen. Lernen heisst ihnen die Runen aufnehmen, die Gliederung der wirklichen Welt anerkennen und adoptiren—lernen, fragen, forschen und kämpfen—das geht bei ihnen allen Hand in Hand : der deutschen Dichtung ist von ältester Zeit her in der Weltliteratur ihre Stellung gegeben als der Poesie des geistigen Kampfes—in der Weltliteratur steht die altgermanische Poesie da als die Poesie des Lernens, des geistigen Wachthums, der geistigen Eroberung."

In a period when the art of writing was practically unknown the aid of rhyme and rhythm was relied upon to preserve the knowledge acquired. Scherer in his *Poetik* (p. 114) says on this point, " Wer in schriftloser Zeit eine Wahrheit in poetische, rhythmische, chorische Form fasste, übergab sie damit dem Gedächtniss in einer für die Aufbewahrung zweckmässigeren Gestalt : man behält Verse leichter als Prosa." Ten Brink in his *Geschichte der englischen Literatur* says further on this point—" Gesetz und Recht, Mythus und Sage, Geschichte und Lebensweisheit wurden auf dem Wege mündlicher Ueber- lieferung in poetischen Sprüchen oder in fluthendem Gesange fortgepflanzt " (p. 14). It is therefore easy to understand how the scop, the professional student and cultivator of the art of poetry, should stand to his hearers in the relation of teacher. Hammerich in his *Altchristliche Epik* (p. 218) writes—" Damals war er nicht allein der Sänger, sondern zugleich der Volks- lehrer in der Religion, der Geschichte, fast in allem was man von göttlichen und menschlichen Dingen wusste." We see him clearly in this light in *Widsith*. The poet is introduced as a man of wide experience.

> "Se þe monna mæst mægþa ofer eorþan
> folca geondferde." (*Widsith* ll. 2-3.)

His first words in the poem are rude maxims in political philosophy.

> " Fela ic monna gefrægn mægþum wealdan ;
> sceal þeodna gehwylc þeawum lifgan,
> eorl æfter oþrum eþle rædan,
> se þe his þeodenstol geþeon wile ! " (*Widsith* ll. 10-13).

In the same poem we have the first bits of general history con- veyed in any Germanic language. It is perhaps interesting in passing to note that just as the study of history often begins in the nursery with noting the great mountain peaks of human achievement (Solomon was the wisest man, Moses was the meek- est man, etc.), of such a character was much of the historical knowledge of the old Germans.

" Þara wæs Hwala hwile selast
and Alexandreas ealra ricost
monna cynnes and he mæst geþah.

  *   *   *   *   *   *

Offa weold Ongle, Alewih Denum
se wæs þara manna modgast ealra."
(Widsith ll. 14-16, and 35-36.)

In the lists of rulers, in the historical sketch of Offa, in the long lists of names of peoples visited we see the poet distinctly in his capacity of teacher and savant.

This didactic tone is common throughout Anglo-Saxon literature. A passage in the Gnomic Verses shows how intimately the art of poetry was associated with learning and wisdom in the Anglo-Saxon mind.

" Ræd sceal mon secgan, rune writan,
leoþ gesingan, lofes gearnian."
(Grein-Wülker, Bibl. I. p. 349, ll. 139-40.)

In the riddle on the Anglo-Saxon scop his function as teacher is expressly mentioned—

"Nu snottre men swiþast lufiaþ
midwist mine : ic monigum sceal
wisdom cyþan." (Ib. III, 238, Riddle 95.)

The following classification (Meyer, Altdeutsche Poesie, 42-45) will afford some idea of the extent to which the poetry of the various branches of the Germanic race of the early centuries of the Christian era is permeated with the didactic spirit. Among the subjects most frequently treated are :

I. The fate of the world in the past and in the future: Voluspa, the smaller Voluspa and the Wessobrunner Gebet.

II. The chief events in the history of the world : Vegtams-kviþa, Heliand, Cynewulf's Christ, the Anglo-Saxon biblical poems Muspilli, Be Dômes Dæge.

III. The present condition of the world : Grimnismal, Vafþrudnismal ; the latter toward the end becomes historic in character.

IV. A catalogue of things : Fafnismal 12-15, Christ, Wonders of Creation, Riddles (A.S.), Meregarto, Physiologus.

V. Ethical and didactic poems : The Gifts of Men, the Monitory Poem (Bi manna mode), the Fragment moral and *religious* (Bi manna lease), the *Fates of Men* (Bi manna wyrdum), *Beowulf*, ll. 1724 *et seq.*

VI. Runes in the Anglo-Saxon *Rune Song.*

VII. Races in *Hyndluljoth.*

VIII. Names in *Voluspa, Grimnismal, Rigsmal, Widsith.*

IX. The best things : *Grimnismal* 43, 44.

X. The naming of things : *Alvissmal.*

Perhaps the only account of the whale given in Anglo-Saxon literature is in verse :

> " Nu ic fitte gen, ymb fisca cynn
> wille woþ-cræfte wordum cyþan
> þurh mod-gemynd, bi þam miclan hwale."
>
> (Cod. Exon. 360, ii. 5-10.)

"I shall teach you through my song" ("ic þe lære þurh leoþorune ") sings Cynewulf in the *Elene*, 1041, 1042.

The Anglo-Saxon takes it for granted that the wise men of old expressed themselves in song. Solomon, the wisest of men, is knowing in songs, "giedda gearo. .snottor." Judas, through whose wisdom the cross is found, is represented in *Elene* as skilled in song. In Cynewulf's *Christ*, wisdom or prudence is mentioned as if it were one of the chief qualifications of the singer—

> " se mæg eal fela
> singan and secgan þam biþ snyttru-cræft
> bifolen on ferþe " (*Christ* 665-667).

How clearly poetry was associated with wisdom in the mind of the Anglo-Saxon is shown in a passage from the poem on the Wonders of Creation.

> " Is þara anra gehwam orgeate tacen,
> þam þurh wisdom woruld ealle con
> behabban on hreþre, hycgende mon
> Þaet geara iu gliwes cræfte
> mid gieddingum guman oft wrecan,
> rincas rædfæste, cuþon ryht sprecan
> þæt a fricgende fira cynnes
> and secgende searoruna gespon
> a gemyndge mæst monna wiston." (*W.* 8-16.)

Poetry being the medium through which knowledge was

imparted, truth became one of its important qualities. The aged Scylding in *Beowulf* sings a song true and sorrowful: "hwilum gyd awræc soþ and sarlic" (ll. 2109, 2110). David is praised in the Kentish Paraphrase as the most truthful singer: "sangere he wæs soþfæstest" (i. 6).

The earliest translations of the Scripture into Anglo-Saxon were poetical. Du Chaillu says of the early Norse tribes, "From their songs the people heard of the birth of their religion, of the creation of the world, of the religion of the past" (*Viking Age*, ii. 389).

It is perhaps worthy of note in this connection that the Minnesingers of several centuries later were looked upon as teachers. The Spielmann, Tristan for instance, instructs the young Isot in the foreign languages, in music and in other branches of learning. (*Trist.* 799.)

The Scop's Power of Memory.

A quickly apprehensive and retentive memory was one of the most important qualifications for the scop's calling. Hrothgar's scop is distinguished by his good memory. He is

"gidda gemyndig
se þe eal-fela eald gesegena
worn gemunde" (*Beow.* 869-871).

In the Gnomic Verses the divinely gifted scop must know many songs.

Among the Scandinavians, the marvellous memory of certain professional singers was a subject of legend. In the *Fornmanna Saga*, c. 6, for instance, the king said, "How many songs hast thou sung now?" Stuf (a blind scald) answered, "I intended that you should count them." "I have done it," said the king, "they are thirty now, but why dost thou sing only flokks? Dost thou not know any drapas?" Stuf answered, "I know fewer drapas than flokks, though many flokks which I know are still unsung." The scalds took pride in reciting for a great length of time without repeating a single poem. In Harald Hardradi we read of an Icelandic scald who had recently arrived at court. "The Icelander began to look sad....the king saw it and asked..... The king answered,

' That is not the reason .... I suspect that thy sagas are now all told.... now thou dost not like the sagas to be wanting during Yule but wilt not tell the same sagas again.' "

Original Composition.

The duty which made the greatest demands upon the genius of the scop was that of original composition. As the warriors were pledged to defend their chief with their lives and to ascribe to him their deeds of valour, so it was the duty of the scop to exalt his fame before the warriors and others assembled in the mead-hall. This function is definitely referred to in *Widsith*. The ideal chieftain, the one who avails himself of the scop's art, is a connoisseur in song, generous in gifts, who wishes to exalt his fame before his warriors, to assert his lordship—

> " gydda gleawne, geofum unhneawne
> seþe fore duguþe wile dom aræran
> eorlscipe æfnan."

Strutt in his book on the *Sports and Pastimes of the Early English*, p. 251, in speaking of a later time says:— " Even the inferior chieftains had their poets to recall their actions and indulge their vanity." In *Beowulf* we get a brief glimpse of the scop at work preparing for the performance of his duty as poet-laureate. He must at the ensuing feast celebrate Beowulf's heroic deed in song—

> " secg eft ongan
> siþ Beowulfes snyttrum styrian
> and on sped wrecan spel gerade " (*Beowulf*, ll. 872-4).

Widsith states expressly that he sang in praise of his queen.

> " Hyre lof lengde geond londa fela,
> þonne ic be songe secgan sceolde,
> hwær ic under swegle selast wisse
> goldhrodene cwen giefe bryttian " (*Widsith*, ll. 99-102).

At the close of the poem the poet refers to this function as one of the most important elements of the power and dignity of his calling.

> " Lof se gewyrceþ,
> hafaþ under heofonum heahfæstne dom " (*Ib*. 142-143).

A taste of this professional flattery of the great is perceptible in the following lines of the same poem :—

> " Swa ic þæt symle onfond on þære feringe,
>   þæt se biþ leofast londbuendum,
>   se þe him god syleþ gumena rice
>   to gehealdenne, þenden he her leofaþ " (*Ib.* 131-134).

The poet singers whom Priscus heard at the court of Attila praised in their songs the mighty deeds and the warlike virtues of their king :

"ᾄσματα πεποιημένα ἔλεγον, νίκας αὐτοῦ καὶ τὰς κατὰ πόλεμον ᾄδοντες ἀρετάς."

The Scop the Historian of his Time.

The scop was the only historian among the early Anglo-Saxons. " It was the minstrel's duty not only to tell the mythic history of the earlier ages but to relate contemporary events and clothe in poetry the deeds which fell under his eye " (Wright, *Biog. Brit.* I, 4). He preserved in song the great deeds, the great events of his time. In a tantalizingly small excerpt given in *Widsith* we have a vivid and suggestive picture of one of the conflicts between the Goths and the Huns, composed probably by a contemporary.

> " Fuloft þær wig ne alæg,
>   þonne Hræda here heardum sweordum
>   ymb Wistlawudu wergan sceoldon
>   ealdne eþelstol Ætlan leodum " (*Widsith*, 119-122).

The historical character of the old Germanic poetry was noticed by Tacitus. He refers to it as the only historical record existing among the Germans. The songs mentioned by Jordanes as sung by the Eastern Goths in the fifth century were clearly historical, " ante quos etiam cantu majorum facta.....canebant " (Jordanes, *loc. cit.*). This tendency to clothe great events in poetical form obtained throughout the entire Anglo-Saxon period. The poem on the Fight at Maldon is an excellent example from the close of the tenth century. The Anglo-Saxon Chronicle contains six historical poems, and in addition to these there are several passages the rhythmic and alliterative character of which suggests that they were paraphrases of historical poems. Wülker in his *Grundriss zur Geschichte der angelsächsichen*

Lit., p. 338, says on this point, "Ausserdem aber zeigen noch gar manche andere Stellen der Chronik Spuren von stabreimenden Versen (bisweilen auch Reimen) oder es erinnert uns die ganze Ausdrucksweise an die Dichtung. Sieben solcher Stellen lassen sich noch mit ziemlicher Sicherheit ausscheiden, wo die Chronikenschreiber teils Lieder hereinarbeiteten oder solche ihrer Darstellung zu Grunde legten. Es sind dies : Gute Zeit unter Eadgar's Herrschaft, 959 (958), Ermordung Eadweard's zu Corfesgeat, 979, Verwüstung Canterbury's, 1011, Eadweard Ætheling, Sohn des Eadmund Irensid, 1057, Margarethe's Vermählung mit Malcolm v. Schottland, 1067, Graf Ralph's verhängnissvolle Hochzeit, 1076 (1075), Wilhelm des Eroberers Herrschaft, 1085 (1087). Doch auch sonst kann man hier und da vermuten, dass Lieder zur Darstellung der Ereignisse benutzt wurden." Our knowledge of the earliest history of the Scandinavians is derived almost entirely from their songs. Du Chaillu, who has made this branch of history a special study, says : "The people looked to their poets to perpetuate in song and transmit to future generations the deeds of their heroes and the fame which was to cling to their names when they had gone to Valhalla.... From these poets or scalds we learn all we know of the history of the earlier Norse tribes " (*Viking Age*, II, 389).

Extemporization.

In addition to these more regular duties it is probable that the scop was called upon by his chief at times to compose and recite upon a given subject with little or no time for preparation. At a period when the art of writing was unknown and the preservation of song and saga depended upon the memory alone, extemporization would naturally constitute a considerable element in much of the recitation. Instances of extempore composition are preserved to us in Scandinavian literature. In the *Flateyjarbok*, III, King Olaf commands Thorfinn, an Icelandic poet, to clothe in poetic form the incidents represented in drawings upon the hangings. Weinhold in his *Altnordisches Leben*, p. 334, gives the following :— "König Harold Hardradi (1047-1066) ging einmal mit dem Skald Thiodolf über die Gasse und hörte wie sich in einem Hause ein Gerber und ein Schmied

zankten. ' Mach mir augenblicks ein Gedicht hierauf,' rief er
dem Dichter zu : ' der eine Kerl sei der Riese Geirröd, der
andere Thor.' Thiodolf stabte sofort einige Weise zusammen
und der König war zufrieden und lobte ihn als guten Skald.''

Criticism of the Time.

It is but natural to suppose that an audience composed
largely of those who were themselves proficient in the singer's
art would be somewhat critical. And such in reality seems to
have been the case, for it is remarkable that even in the meagre
details that have come down to us concerning the Anglo-Saxon
scop mention should be made of one who was dismissed from
his office to make room for one of superior skill, '' leoþcræftig
mann.'' From *Widsith* we learn that many of the chiefs among
the ancient Germans were connoisseurs in song :—

> '' simle suþ oþþe norþ sumne gemetaþ
>
> gydda gleawne '' (*Widsith*, 138-139).

The critical spirit with which the scop's audience sometimes
listened to his performance is indicated in the same poem. The
poet, after mentioning how he and Scilling raised the song to
the accompaniment of the harp in the presence of their victor-
ious lord, refers to the effect of their recital upon the audience
and states that many men severely critical in disposition (that I
take to be in this connection the meaning of '' modum wlonce,''
literally '' proud in mind '') said that they had never heard a
better song :—

> '' Þonne monige men modum wlonce
>
> wordum sprecan, þaþe wel cuþan,
>
> þæt hi næfre song sellan ne hyrdon.''

The Scop in War.

We have no direct evidence in Anglo-Saxon literature that
the scop in his professional character accompanied the warriors
upon their expeditions, but our knowledge of the social conditions of those times, the known customs of related peoples, and
one or two historical incidents of the later Anglo-Saxon period
render the existence of such a custom not improbable. In some
of the passages from Anglo-Saxon literature already quoted the

scop is spoken of as a warrior, and it is probable that he upon occasion engaged in the battle side by side with those to whom he sang. It is quite likely that in the primitive society of the time of which we speak the profession of arms was by no means so clearly differentiated from that of song as we of a more highly organized civilization are likely to think.

Among the Scandinavians the scalds went to battle occasionally, not as warriors but as singers. In the *Fostbroedra Saga*, p. 47, it is said of King Olaf, " He then called his scalds and bid them go into the shieldburg, ' You shall stay here,' said the king ' and see what takes place and then no saga is needed to tell you afterwards what you shall make songs about ' " (Du Chaillu, *Viking Age*, II, 393).

Although as already has been intimated it is quite likely that the scop was frequently on the battlefield as a warrior, it is extremely doubtful that he ever sang songs there as did the Norman minstrel at the battle of Hastings. On this point Kögel (*Geschichte d. deutsch. Lit.* I, i, 18) says :— " Ob die später bezeugte Sitte eines Vorsängers beim Zuge in die Schlacht schon der ältesten Zeit zugeschrieben werden darf ist zweifelhaft." The fact that Alfred should venture into the Danish camp in the disguise of a harper is proof that the Anglo-Saxon and Danish warriors of this time were accustomed to find entertainment in music and song. The singers, however, apparently amused the leisure of the soldiers rather than incited them to battle.

The Scop as Traveller.

Various passages in Anglo-Saxon literature indicate that the scop was accustomed to travel. The custom is expressly referred to, for instance, in Widsith.

" Swa scriþende gesceapum hweorfaþ
    gleomen gumena geond grunda fela " (*Widsith*, 135-136).
The very name of the scop, Widsith, seems to reveal an association in the minds of the old Germans between the scop's profession and distant journeyings. The statement made concerning him in the introduction to the poem,

      " seþe monna mæst mærþa ofer eorþan
      folca geondferde " (*Widsith*, 2-3),

and the long lists of geographical names given suggest that it
was a great distinction to have travelled widely.   Another passage in the same poem indicates quite distinctly that to have seen
many lands, to have had a wide and varied experience was considered a qualification for the poet-singer's calling.   After stating
that he had passed through many strange lands and had endured
the vicissitudes and privations of one who travels widely, he con-
tinues, " Therefore I may sing and recite tales before the com-
pany in the mead-hall."

" Swa ic geondferde fela fremdra londa
geond ginne grund, godes and yfles
þær ic cunnade cnosle bidæled :
freomægum feor folgade wide.
Forþon ic mæg singan and secgan spell,
mænan fore mengo in meoduhalle," etc. (*Widsith*, 50-55.)

An investigation of the conditions under which the scop
practised his art reveals some good reasons for the existence of
this custom.   Remaining always at his post, singing ever before
the same restricted circle of hearers, the songs of the most re-
sourceful of poets would sooner or later pall upon the taste.
" Aber nicht immer verweilte der Sänger an ein und demselben
Fürstenhofe.   Es lag in der Natur der Sache dass er seine
Lieder nicht immer wieder vor demselben kleinen Kreise in der
Methalle seines Königes vortragen konnte und mochte, dass er
daher nach einem Publikum suchte " (Vogt, *Leben u. Dicht. d.
Spielmänner*, 5).   On his journeys the scop was able to obtain
not only material for songs new and strange to those at home,
but possibly suggestions for rendering this material in new and
attractive form.   It is also not to be overlooked that the scop
found on his travels audiences to whom his old songs were new
and interesting.

Koehler (*Germania*, XV, p. 43) ascribes considerable importance to the fact that these journeys would bring the scop
into touch with others of the profession.   " Der Verkehr mit
anderen Berufsgenossen war aber für die Sänger eine Noth-
wendigkeit, damit ihnen neue Sagenstoffe zugeführt wurden
und sie nicht auf einen engen Kreis von Liedern, die allen durch
oftmaliges Anhören längst geläufig waren, beschränkt blieben,

sondern eine reiche Fülle männigfältiger Gedichte ihnen zu Ge-
bote stand, so dass die Zuhörer einer erfreulichen Abwechslung
geniessen konnten." Ten Brink (*Gesch. d. eng. Lit.* I, 15)
ascribes the custom to that fondness for travel so characteristic
of the Anglo-Saxon even to-day. " Seine Kunst trägt ihm hohes
Lob und reiche Gaben ein. Trotzdem ergreift ihn [den Scop]
oft die Sehnsucht nach der Ferne, der germanische Wander-
trieb, und von Hofe zu Hofe reisend bringt er, überall ein gern
gesehener Gast, neue Lieder und Kunde von fremden Völkern
und neuen Ereignissen mit." The many attractions of such a
wandering existence, the constant changes of scene, the ever
new and attentive audiences, the variety of experience, and the
occasional rich rewards, led some of the poet-singers to adopt it
as a permanent mode of life. One of the riddles in Grein's
collection has for its subject such a singer. In it he is mentioned as singing for the most part before strangers,

" fereþ wide

and me fremdes ær freondum stondeþ
hiþendra hyht "

(*Bibliothek d. angelsäch. Poesie*, III, 238, No. 95).

Other Occasional Functions of the Scop.

The travelling scop performed other functions than those
directly associated with the practice of his art. As intimated in
the passages just quoted from Ten Brink the news which he had
gathered on his journeys and the knowledge which he had
acquired of many lands and peoples made him a doubly welcome
guest in court and hall. The news was imparted directly or in
the songs with which the scop entertained his audience. It
was, for instance, through the songs of the wandering singer
that Beowulf learned of the devastation wrought in Heorot by
the monster Grendel—

"forþam syþþan wearþ

ylda bearnum undyrne cuþ
gyddum geomore, þætte Grendel wan
hwile wiþ Hroþgar " (*Beow.* 149-152).

Scherer (*Poetik*, p. 122) refers to the wandering singer of a later
time as " der fahrende Sänger, der Spielmann, welcher im
Mittelalter die Rolle des Journalisten spielt."

This wandering life led by the singers, their wide acquaintance with countries and peoples, and a certain immunity from molestation, which as we have elsewhere shown (*e.g. Lex Frisionum*, p. 11 of this paper) they enjoyed, fitted them admirably for service as messengers. And they seem to have been employed in this capacity, although no direct mention is made of this in Anglo-Saxon literature. It is suggestive to note in this connection, however, that in the *Nibelungenlied* Etzel's Spielmänner are sent as messengers. On this phase of the activity of the Spielmänner of the early middle ages Grimm writes : " Werbel und Swemmlein, Etzel's Spielleute, sind aus dem Nibelungenlied bekannt. Sie erfreuen sich grosser Gaben und werden als Boten am Rhein ehrenvoll empfangen und behandelt . . Die Spielleute dienten zugleich als Boten, wie eben jener bei Saxo. Hierzu taugten sie vorzugsweise weil sie durch ihre Reisen pflegten aller Orten bekannt zu sein und ihre Kunst freien Zutritt verschaffte......Spielmann Isung wird (*Vilkina saga* c. 118) von einem Könige an den anderen als Bote gesendet und dabei die Bemerkung gemacht, dass Spielleute im Frieden überall sogar dahin reisen konnten, wo andere Verdacht erregen würden " (*Deutsche Heldensage*, p. 283). On the same point Weinhold (*Deutsche Frauen*, ii, 131) writes : " Beim Weiterziehen wurden sie oft mit einer Botschaft betraut, denn in Genusse eines besonderen Friedens waren sie die sichersten Gesandten."

It may be well to note here also that the travelling singers of the 12th century and of a much earlier time were employed to publish not only heroic but also shameful deeds. " Auch erhielten sie [die Spielleute] wohl den Auftrag eine That von besonderer Ruhmwürdigkeit oder Schande zu verbreiten und gemein zu machen ; sie waren der öffentliche Mund ihrer Zeit. Jenes Botenamt und dieses Scheltenamt haftete ihnen so fest an, dass es noch auf ihre niedrigeren Nachfolger, die Fahrenden, überging. * * * * Spielmänner und Spielweiber wurden zu Boten (*Parz.* 362,21, *Nibel.* 1347), Dichter und Spielleute zu Scheltern gebraucht, welche Ehre und Schande je nach dem Auftrage ausbreiteten " (Weinhold, *Deutsche Frauen*, II, 131). A passage in Iwein refers to this custom—

"si muosen vaste gelten vür des Todes schelten
und vür die scheltaere boeser geltaere" (*Iwein*, 7162-28).

In his note on this passage Lachmann says—"Diese Zeilen erhalten ihr volles Licht aus dem, was in J. Grimm's *Rechtsalterthümer*, s. 953, nachgetragen ist. Statt dass man jetzt gewöhnlich nur droht, den Namen des wortbrüchigen Schuldners in den Zeitungen an den Pranger zu stellen, bediente man sich, wie wir hier sehen, in früheren Zeiten der scheltaere, und dieses Amt übernahmen die herumziehenden Sänger." Diodorus Siculus mentions a similar practice as existing among the bards. (*Bibliotheca Historica*, lib. V, c. 31).

Rank and Influence of the Scop.

The scop held among the early Anglo-Saxons a position of honour. The simplicity of their social organization, the immediate relations in which one member of the tribe stood to the others gave the incumbent of this office a weight and influence which it is difficult to imagine. "In alten Zeiten," says Scherer (*Poetik*, 180), "stehen die epischen Sänger am Hofe des Königs als gleichberechtigt neben dem Gefolge: es wurde ihnen ein grosser Platz eingeräumt, denn sie waren mit dem König und mit dem Volk intim." Widsith assumes towards kings and rulers the tone of an adviser—

"sceal þeodna gehwylc þeawum lifgan
eorl æfter oþrum eþle rædan
seþe his þeodenstol geþeon wile" (*Widsith*, 11-13).

Koehler (*Germania*, XV) considers it significant that in *Beowulf*, 2105, the king should be "unmittelbar neben dem Sänger genannt."

The scop possessed the power of increasing the prestige of a chief in the eyes of his subjects.

"Gleomen . . . . .

. . . .
simle suþ oþþe norþ sumne gemetaþ
se þe for duguþe wile dom aræran,
eorlscipe æfnan." (*Widsith*, 136-141.)

He then asserts the great value of the poet's services—

" lof se gewyrceþ

hafaþ under heofonum heahfæstne dom." (*Ib.* 142-143.)

From the Anglo-Saxon riddle on the scop (Grein, *Bibl. d. a. s. Poesie* III, No. 95) we learn that the scop was famous among the people "folcum gefrǣge." The same authority informs us that his society was much sought after by the wisest in the nation.

" Nu snottre men swiþast lufiaþ

midwiste mine."

The importance of the scop in early Anglo-Saxon society is emphasized in the *Gnomic Verses*. " Just as jewels are suitable for a queen," says the poet, "a weapon for enemies, so is a good scop for men,"

" sinc on cwene

god scop gumum, garniþwerum " (*Gnomic Verses*, 127-128).

The extraordinary talent for composition and song which distinguished the scop was looked upon as a divine gift. Thus in the *Gnomic Verses*—

Ƿy læs þe him con leoþa worn

oþþe mid hondum con hearpan gretan

hafaþ him his gliwes gife þe him god sealde."

(*Ib.* 170-172.)

Cynewulf refers to his poetic gifts in the same way—" mægencyning * * breostlocan onwand, leoþucræft onleac " (*Elene*, 1249-50).

The poet-singers among the early Anglo-Saxons seem to have borne significant names, which would not have been the case had they not occupied positions of considerable importance and prominence. Müllenhof has made an interesting study of this subject; he writes :—" Göttern und göttlichen Wesen sind in allen Mythologien besonders bedeutsame Namen beigelegt. Dieselbe Ehre ward Sängern zu Theil. Wir finden bei den Griechen die Namen Phemios, Demodokos, Musaios, Eumolpos, Hesiodos, Lesches, Terpandros, Stesichoros und andere, die alle auf die Kunst oder den Stand und die Lebensweise der Dichter hinweisen ; ebenso bei den Angelsachsen den weitgereisten Sänger Vîdsîd und seinen Genossen Scilling

(v. ahd. scellan). Deor muss wie hildedeor, heathodeor verstanden werden, vergl. Grimm zu *Andreas*, 1002. Etzels Spielmänner heissen Werbel und Swemmel; jenes wird ahd. Hwerbilo sein und "gyrovagus" bedeuten, dieses muss man auf Sweimilo zurückführen wie Hemmi, Hemmilo auf Heimo, Heimrih. Morolt, als er in Spielmannsweise einherzieht, nennt sich Stolzelin. Seit den 12ten und 13ten Jahrhunderten sind bekannt die Dichternamen, der Glichsære, Spervogel, Vridanc, der Strickære, Vrouwenlop, Muscatplüt, Rosenplüt und andere. Die lange Dauer des Gebrauchs solcher Namen lässt schliessen, dass schon die Sänger des altdeutschen Epos ähnliche, dem edlern und höhern Stil der alten Poesie gemäss gebildete wie bei den Angelsachsen trugen." (*Zeitschrift f. d. A.*, VII, 530.)

The Frisians, the immediate neighbours of the Anglo-Saxons on the mainland, who probably resembled them as closely in their laws and social customs as in their language, esteemed the harpers so highly that they accorded them especial legal protection. The following is an extract from their laws dating probably from the 8th century. "Qui harpatorem, qui cum circulo harpare potest, in manum percusserit, componat illud quarta parte majore compositione quam alteri ejusdem conditionis homini; aurifici similiter; foeminae fresum facienti similiter" (*Monumenta Germanica Historica, Leges* 3).

The art of music, song and story was one which kings themselves did not disdain to cultivate. Hrothgar, the king of the Danes, takes the harp at the feast and recites in song curious tales of bygone times.

> "Þær wæs gidd and gleo : gomela Scilding
> fela fricgende feorran rehte ;
> hwilum hilde-deor hearpan wynne,
> gomen-wudu grette, hwilum gyd awræc
> soþ and sarlic : hwilum syllic spell
> rehte æfter rihte rum-heort cyning."
>
> (*Beow.* 2106-2111.)

Scherer writes in this connection, "Der epische Sänger ist ein angesehener Mann den wir in den Resten unseres Epos selbst wiederfinden. Er ist ein Gefolgsmann des Königs geehrt, gelobt und beschenkt wie ein Held. Und auch der Held und König verschmäht es nicht, seine Kunst zu üben" (*Gesch. d. deut. Dicht. in 11. und 12. Jahrh.* p. 31). Müllenhof holds the same opinion, "Aber darum war er [der Scop] nicht weniger als irgend ein anderer Mann eines Königs : Könige und Helden dieser Zeit übten selbst den Gesang, und dieser stand mit dem gesammten Heldenleben im nächsten Zusammenhange" (*Sagen aus Schles.-Holstein*, ix). Widsith refers to the kings of his time who were connoisseurs in song, "gydda gleawne." Even in the late Anglo-Saxon period we find frequent mention of men of noble or royal rank who were skilled in the scop's art. Among others Dunstan, Aldhelm and Alfred, King Horn (ed. Wissmann 1485) and Hereward (Michel, *Chron. Norm.* II, 19) are represented in the old ballads bearing their names as composing and singing and accompanying themselves with the harp. History and saga furnish instances of princes of other Teutonic races who were proficient in poetry and music. Procopius (*Bell. Vandal.* 2, 6) relates that Gelimer the king of the Vandals in his captivity begged for a harp that he might bewail his misfortunes.

In some instances we have specific mention of the fact that the scop himself was of noble descent. Widsith belonged to the noble race of the Myrgings.

" Him from Myrgingum
æþelo onwocon."

In *Beowulf* (l. 868) the scop is a king's thane.

" hwilum cyninges þegn
guma gilphlæden."

Deor as scop had held a grant of land from his king and hence ranked as a thane. Widsith likewise received grants of land not only from his king but also from his queen.

" Þæsþe he me lond forgeaf,
mines fæder eþel, frea Myrginga,
and me þa Ealhhild oþerne forgeaf,
dryhtcwen duguþe " (ll. 95-98).

The character of the poetry which has been handed down to us from the ancient Anglo-Saxon is in itself evidence of his rank. It is exclusively aristocratic; the common people are seldom mentioned. We are impressed with the ceremonious

dignity with which the different characters in *Beowulf* act.
Widsith introduces us to the great kings and heroes of his race,
and the unfortunate and melancholy Deor finds consolation in
comparing his fate with that of the most exalted characters in
myth and saga.   Wars are spoken of as taking place between
chiefs and nobles rather than between peoples.   Only in *Beowulf* (2472) and perhaps in the struggle between the Frisians
and the Danes is national feeling traceable.   " In der Regel,"
says Meyer (*Alt. Germ. Poesie*, 52), " wird das Volk in der alt-
germanischen Poesie vertreten durch den König mit seiner
Umgebung, den Hof."   Koehler (*Germania*, XV, 110) notes as
a further indication of the social position of the scop, " Widsith
. . . sucht die besten und verzüglichsten Helden der königlichen
Gefolge auf."   At banquets the scop was usually seated near the
king, a position of honour in the punctilious etiquette of the
time.   In the poem on " The Fates of Men " the scop is spoken
of as sitting at the feet of the king.

" Sum sceal mid hearpan æt his hlafordes
fotum sittan, feoh þicgan " (ll. 73-74).

Gustav Freytag in an article in the *Grenzboten*, 1866, p. 30,
writes :— " Wenn die Magen und Mannen auf der Methbank
ihres Hauptlings sassen, dann hatte er (der Sänger) einen
Ehrenplatz zu den Füssen des Wirthes."

Conditions which Account for his Influence.

The dignity and worth of the scop stand out in marked con-
trast to the disrepute of their degenerate successors of later
times.   The respect and consideration with which these singers
were treated in the early Anglo-Saxon period may be attributed
to various causes.   First, the singer was not only a man distinguished by his skill in almost the only fine art which the
Anglo-Saxon cultivated, but he was the curator of their literature and of their religious and historical myths, and something
of the religious character of the primitive poetry adhered to the
professional singer.   " Die alte Dichtkunst war ein heiliges, zu
den Göttern unmittelbar in Bezug stehendes, mit Weissagung
und Zauber zusammenhängendes Geschäft " (J. Grimm,
Deutsche Myth. II, 749).   In the oldest High German texts

the word "scof" is used to translate "psalmista," "psaltes,"
"vates."   When the Anglo-Saxon read or wrote of sacred Biblical characters his imagination represented these in the figure
of the scop.   Cynewulf thinks of Moses as a singer—
> " myhta wealdend be tham Moses sang "

> *(Elene,* 337).

In another passage of the same poem the prophets are conceived
of as singers—
> " hu on worulde ær witgan sungon
>   gasthalige guman be godes bearne " (*Elene,* 561-2).

The scop in *Beowulf* possesses some traces of priestly character:
> " þær wæs hearpan sweg
>   swutol sang scopes, sægde se þe cuþe
>   Frumsceaft fira feorran reccan
>   cwæþ thæt se almihtiga eorþan worhte " (ll. 89-92).

In the *Monitory Poem* the prophet is spoken of as singing—
> " Ʋæt se witga song
>   gearowyrdig guma and þæt gyd awræc."

> *(Grein-Wülker,* III, p. 146, ll. 50-51.)

Again in the *Phoenix,*
> " þus frod guma on fyrndagum
>   gieddade gleawmod godes spellboda,
>   ymb his æriste in ece lif " (*Ib.* p. 113, ll. 570-3).

The high esteem in which the scop was held by the king
was probably due in part to the fact that the singer exerted a
powerful influence upon public opinion.   Scherer emphasizes
this point:— " Von unschätzbarem Werth ist die Poesie für
diejenigen, welche mittelst ihrer den Willen zu beherrschen
wünschen.   Die Poesie schärft die Tugenden ein, welche den
Machthabern erwünscht sind.   * * *   Was schärft das germanische ein?   Was die Volkskönige von ihren Unterthanen ver-
langen, erwarten : Tapferkeit, Treue.   Es singt den Ruhm der
sangliebenden Könige der Völkerwanderung : es preist den
Mann der sich in edler Aufopferung für seinen Herrn hingiebt,
der einen ruhmvollen Tod höher achtet als ein schmachvolles
Leben " (*Poetik,* 119).

But that which more than anything else won for the singer
the favour of the great was the power he possessed of extending

through his songs the fame of those whom he praised. One of life's greatest prizes to the Angle or Saxon was great renown as a warrior and leader. Personal valour and prowess on the field of battle, courage in times of danger, hardihood in endurance, these were the all-absorbing topics of conversation in the mead-hall. He whose achievements were the subject of general discussion enjoyed one of valour's sweetest rewards. That the influence exercised by the scop was recognized by the princes of the time, that his services were sought for and rewarded is plainly implied in a passage from *Widsith* already quoted :—

> " Simle suþ oþþe norþ sumne gemetaþ
> gydda gleawne, geofum unhneawne,
> se þe fore duguþe wile dom aræran,
> eorlscipe æfnan."

The same poet states concerning Ealhhilde, his queen, who had been especially gracious to him, that he extended her fame throughout many lands :—

> " Hyre lof lengde geond londa fela,
> þonne ic be songe secgan sceolde,
> hwær ic under swegle selast wisse
> goldhrodene cwen giefe bryttian "   (ll. 99-102).

Dress and Instruments.

Jacob Grimm favours the opinion that the court singers wore a peculiar dress. "In Ländern und Zeiten die der Dichtkunst hold waren, darf man auch den Sängern, namentlich den Höfischen, eigenthümliche Tracht zutrauen " (*Deutsche Mythologie*, p. 862). He makes, however, no citations in support of this opinion. The gleemen depicted in Anglo-Saxon manuscript illustrations are not to be distinguished in dress from the ordinary citizen.

The harp was the instrument most used by the scop. It was used by Widsith to accompany his song, "hlude bi hearpan hleoþor swinsade." And it is frequently mentioned in *Beowulf*. It is almost invariably referred to in terms that show that it was an instrument in the music of which the Anglo-Saxons took especial delight. " þaer waes hearpan sweg," is a feature in the description of the hall joys at Heorot. " Nis þær hearpan sweg" (*Beow.* 2458), describes a condition of sorrow and desolation, so also does the line "nalles hearpan sweg wigend weccean" (*Beow.* 3023). The use of the instrument to accompany song or recitative is frequently referred to in *Beowulf*—

> "hwilum hildedeor hearpan wynne,
> gomenwudu grette, hwilum gyd awræc" (l. 2107).

In a passage already quoted Jordanes refers to the use by the Goths of the harp to accompany song. "Ante quos etiam cantu majorum facta modulationibus citharisque canebant" (*supra*, p. 8). Venantius Fortunatus already in the sixth century recognizes the harp as a peculiarly German instrument—

> "Romanusque lyra, plaudat tibi barbarus harpa,
> Nos tibi versiculos, dent barbara carmina leudos
> Sic variante tropo laus sonet una viro."

The Anglo-Saxons seem to have cultivated the use and manufacture of this instrument with especial care, for according to De Coussemaker (*Ann. Archéol.* ix, 289) this instrument was generally known on the continent in the ninth century as the "cithara anglica." A peculiar form of the instrument known as the "Swalwe" was also invented in England :

> "Swalwen, diu noch z'Engellant,
> z'einer tiwern härpfen ist erkant" (*Parzival*, 663, 17).

Perhaps the oldest representation of the Anglo-Saxon harp that is preserved to us is contained in a manuscript of the eighth century in the British Museum. It is simply an oblong board containing in the upper half an aperture of the same shape. Across this longitudinally are stretched six strings. The instrument as it appears in manuscripts of two centuries later has a highly developed form. In an illustration in the so called Cædmon MS. of the tenth century preserved in the Bodleian Library at Oxford, the harp has a form approximating to that of a right-angled triangle. The Anglo-Saxon poetical names for the harp, "gleo-beam" and "gomenwudu," suggest that wood was used in its construction. The instrument as used by the Anglo-Saxons seldom exceeded three feet in length. While performing the player was seated and held the harp in his lap. There are few if any exceptions to this posture in the earliest

Anglo-Saxon illustrations.   A passage in the Anglo-Saxon poem, *The Fates of Men*, represents the harper as seated during his performance—

> " Sum sceal mid hearpan æt his hlafordes
> fotum sittan " (vv, 80-1).

Circumstances under which the Scop usually Performed.

The feasts given by the Germanic chieftains of the first centuries of the Christian era to their warriors were the centre of the social life of the time.   Tacitus states that the Germans considered these occasions as peculiarly suitable for the transaction of business; reconciliations were brought about, marriages were planned, even proposals of peace or war were discussed. At no other time, they thought, was man so true-hearted, so susceptible to the influence of lofty thoughts.   " Sed et de reconciliandis invicem inimicis et iungendis affinitatibus et asciscendis principibus, de pace denique ac bello plerumque in conviviis consultant, tanquam nullo magis tempore aut ad simplices cogitationes pateat animus aut ad magnas incalescat " (*Germania*, 22).

It was on these occasions especially that the old Germans indulged in the highest artistic enjoyment which their civilization afforded them, that of music, song and story.   Sometimes the harp was passed from hand to hand as Bæda tells us in the Cædmon story.   But the chief performance was that of the professional singer or scop.   He usually occupied a seat of honour near the king and remained seated while reciting his poems, accompanying himself with the harp.

Manner of Delivery.

The tones of the harp were probably used to mark the emphatic alliterative syllables.   Comparetti, in his work on the Kalevala, states that this is the method of accompaniment among the Finns, whose customs in recent times present many interesting analogies to those of the Anglo-Saxons.   " Harfenaccorde stützten die Stabreime, das übrige wurde mit gehobener Stimme deklamiert, kaum in eigentlicher Melodie gesungen " (Comparetti, *Kalevala*, German translation, p. 65).

The performance of the scop differed considerably from singing in our sense of the term. The expression so common in early Germanic literature, "singan and secgan," is in this connection significant. Widsith, for instance, says, "Forþon ic mæg singan and secgan spell" (l. 54). The ideas of saying and singing are again associated in the same poem, "þonne ic be songe secgan sceolde" (l. 100). Grein (ii, p. 453) gives four examples of the occurrence of the formula in Anglo-Saxon and still another for "cweþan and singan." In the old Saxon *Heliand* the formula is extended, "settian endi singian endi seggian forth" (*Heliand* I, 33). The frequent use of this formula indicates that the distinct communication of the subject-matter was of greater importance than the merely musical element and that the recitation of the scop was something intermediate between "singing" and "saying," something similar perhaps to chanting or recitative. Some hint of this is given in the history of certain words. The word "siggwan" meant originally "to recite." The word is used by Ulfilas to indicate the reading of the holy scriptures. In the Weissenburger Catechism the prayer is sung. "Gid," the word used frequently to indicate the song of the scop, is from "giddian" which meant "to speak." In *Beowulf* this is used as a synonym for "leoþ," a song. "Leoþ wæs asungen, gleomannes gyd" (l. 1160). Moreover, the metre of old Germanic poetry was such as to preclude its being sung in our sense of the word. It would be impossible to suit the verses to any definite series of musical notes and this is true of even the most lyrical of Anglo-Saxon poems, such, for instance, as *Deor's Complaint*. In the development of the art of song the relative importance of the musical and literary elements has been reversed. With us the text is often little more than a framework for the music; with the Anglo-Saxons the music was but one of the ornamental features of the rendition of the all important narrative. Müllenhof in his introductory essay on the Holsteinish sagas, p. ix., writes:—
" Da der thatsächliche, epische Inhalt, das Wort, Hauptsache ist, war das Singen jedoch mehr ein Sagen als Gesang in unserem Sinne; beide Ausdrücke werden in der alten Kunstsprache verbunden und sind fast gleichbedeutend."

If the style of delivery was something quite different from modern singing it was something quite different also from the ordinary speaking tones of the voice. The adjectives used in Anglo-Saxon in describing the scop's performance indicate that the voice was high and clear. For instance, in *Beowulf* the expression " swutol sang.scopes," and in the same poem the use of the word "hador " (defined by Grein as serenus, limpidus, clarus, splendidus), "scop hwilum sang hâdor on Heorot," evidently refer to something more than ordinary speech. Still clearer evidence of this is afforded in *Widsith* where two singers with clear voices raise the song,

" wit Scilling sciran reorde

. . . . . . song ahofan " (ll. 103-104).

The fact that the harp was so frequently used is in itself evidence that the poet employed something else than the tones of ordinary speech. The scop's performance seems to have been a sort of poetical declamation in which the singing tones were not so prominent as to veil distinctness of utterance, but which, combined with the emotional tone-inflections and the instrumental accompaniment, served to give a musical and artistic effect to the whole. Koegel expresses his opinion on this point as follows :—" Ich möchte aber glauben dass das Ganze auf eine Art Melodram hinauslief. Die Worte des Gedichts wurden langsam und schwerwuchtig mit pathetisch gehobener Stimme recitiert. Dazu erklangen Harfentöne, die durch ihre rhythmische und harmonische Bewegung den ethischen Inhalt der Worte vertiefen sollten " (*Gesch. d. d. Lit.* I, i, 143). Weinhold (*Die deutsche Frauen*) expresses a similar opinion :—" Auf eines muss hier nachdrücklich hingewiesen werden, dass nämlich unsere alte Dichtung nicht gelesen sondern gesagt und gesungen ward, d. h. sie war auf den getragenen, in melodischem Tonwechsel sich bewegenden Vortrag berechnet, der von selbst strophenmässige Abtheilungen forderte. Dieser Gesang konnte entweder ganz frei schweben oder durch sehr einfache Instrumentalbegleitung gestützt werden."

The effectiveness of the scop's primitive art was heightened by several circumstances which have already been noted. One of the most important of these was that at that time the functions of poet, composer and singer were united in one person. The poem on being sung did not lose anything from that greater or less want of sympathy and mutual understanding which is certain to exist when the author and singer are different persons. The poet sang his own poem and found expression for his thoughts and emotions not merely in words but in tone of voice, in play of feature and in gesture. " Hierzu kommt aber noch eines was eine unaussprechliche Tragweite hatte : nämlich dass er selbst und persönlich seine Gesänge dem Volk singend vor- trug " (Hammerich, *Christliche Epik*, p. 219).

The Scop's Rewards.

The singers, like the other members of the primitive court of the early Germanic chieftains, were dependent for their sus- tenance upon the gifts which the generosity or prudence of the chieftain prompted him to give. It is, therefore, but natural that the specimens of scop-poetry still preserved should contain frequent references to the generosity of the chiefs and the rewards received by singers. No mention is made in *Beowulf* of the bestowal of presents upon the scop. The only indications of the existence of such a custom are the abundant references to the king as a giver :—brytta, sinces brytta, goldes brytta, gold-gifa, sinc-gifa, etc. In *Widsith*, on the other hand, where the singer himself is the subject of the poem, the references to the gifts received by him are very numerous. In the very first lines it is stated—

" oft he on flette geþah
mynelicne maþþum " (ll. 3-4).

And in the poem itself the scop in three different passages sings of the gifts which were given him.

The presents mentioned in the earliest texts were usually of gold. The word " maþþum " in the lines just quoted is used in *Beowulf* as a synonym for gold.

" Me þone wælræs wine Scildunga
fættan golde fela leanode,
manegum maþþum " (ll. 2102-2104).

Cynewulf in speaking of his experience as a wandering singer states that he received presents of gold.

"þeah he in meadohealle maþmas þege,
æplede gold " (*Elene*, 1258-1259).

The gold was usually in the form of rings such as bracelets,
arm-rings, collars. The poetical name for chief, "beag-gifa,"
ring-giver, shows how frequently the gifts took this form. In
the brief poem *Widsith* alone there are three references to gifts
of this kind. One of these is interesting in that it is probably
the only instance in Anglo-Saxon poetry in which the exact
value of the gift is stated.

"Se me beag forgeaf burgwarena fruma,
on þam siexhund wæs smætes goldes
gescyred sceaþa scillingrime " (ll. 90-92).

We have direct evidence that two of the Anglo-Saxon scops
held grants of lands from the king. These grants would serve
to attach the singer permanently to the court of his benefactor
and would give him the standing of a thane. The land held by
Deor seems to have been attached to the office of scop and to
have passed with the latter into the hands of his successful
rival, Heorrenda.

"* * * Oþþæt Heorrenda nu,
leodcræftig monn, londryht geþah,
þæt me eorla hleo ær gesealde " (*D. Complaint* 39).

Widsith received grants of land not only from his king but
from his queen also.

" And me þa Ealhhild oþerne (eþel) forgeaf " (l. 97).

As to the value of the presents received by the scop it is to
be noted that Widsith's were so considerable that on his return
he handed them over to his king just as Beowulf did with the
rich presents which Hrothgar had given him.

" Þone ic Eadgilse on æht sealde,
minum hleodryhtne þa ic to ham bicwom
leofum to leane " (ll. 93-95).

This and the fact just noted that Deor, Heorrenda and Widsith
received grants of land favour the opinion that the art of the
ancient scop was richly rewarded. Ten Brink holds this view.
" Seine Kunst trägt ihm hohes Lob und reiche Gaben ein "
(*Gesch. d. e. Lit.* p. 15).

But the gifts though occasionally of great value were by no

means certain. This led naturally to frequent endeavours on the part of the scop to excite the generosity of the patron. This personal appeal of the singer, direct or indirect, open or covert, is one of the peculiarities that distinguish the poetry of this early period from that of the later period of writers and readers. It is, then, possibly, a habit acquired in the days when he was a wandering singer that leads Cynewulf in his earliest written poem to appeal to his readers for a reward, not, indeed, for their gold or silver but for their prayers.

> " Nu ic þonne bidde beorn, se þe lufige
> þysses giddes begang, þæt he geomrum me
> þone halgan heap helpe bidde."
>
> (*Fates of the Apostles*, 88-90.)

The poetic names for king or chief such as "sinces brytta" (*Beow.* 607, 1170, 1922, 2071), "beaga brytta" (*Beow.* 35, 352, 1487) and "beag gyfa," or "sinc gifa" (*Beow.* 2311, 1342, 1012 ; *Guthlac* 1326) speak much for the attitude of the singer toward his patron. They are intended to be not merely epithets of praise but also reminders of duty. Even the hall in which the scop sang is called the ring-hall, "beah-sele." Few qualities of a hero's character are so frequently referred to as is his generosity. Hrothgar possesses this virtue.

> " He beot ne aleh, beagas dælde " (*Beow.* 80).
>
> " Swa manlice mære þeoden
> hord-weard hæleþa heaþo-ræsas geald
> mearum and maþmum swa hy næfre man lyhþ
> se þe secgan wile soþ æfter rihte " (*Beow.* 1046-1049).

Upon Beowulf's return to his own land both he and the king, Hygelac, distinguish themselves by the magnificent gifts which they exchange. The poem *Widsith* abounds in references to particular acts of generosity. Of Guthhere the poet sings—

> "þær ic beag geþah
> me þær Guþhere forgeaf glædlicne maþþum
> songes to leane ; næs þæt sæne cyning " (ll. 65-67).

He then mentions Aelfwine—

> " mid Ælfwine
> se hæfde moncynnes mine gefræge
> leohteste hond lofes to wyrcenne,

> heortan unhneaweste hringa gedales,
> beorhtra beaga " (ll. 70-74).

Concerning Eormanric's liberality Widsith goes into interesting details—

> " þær me Gotena cyning gode dohte
> se me beag forgeaf, burgwarena fruma
> on þam siexhund wæs smætes goldes
> gescyred sceatta scillingrime "   (ll. 89-92).

The passage in which he speaks of Ealhhild's generosity and of his gratitude seems to be a recommendation by the poet of himself as one who spreads far and wide the fame of those who bestow gifts upon him.   A similar subtle hint that the singer's art be encouraged by generosity seems traceable in the opening lines of *Beowulf.*

> "Beowulf wæs breme (blæd wide sprang)
> Scyldes eafera Scede-landum in.
> Swa sceal geong guma gode gewyrcean,
> fromum feoh-giftum on fæder wine,
> þæt hine on ylde eft gewunigen
> wil gesiþas, þonne wig cume,
> leode gelæsten ; lof-dædum sceal
> in mægþa gehwære man geþeon ! " (*Beow.* 18-25).

Conclusion.

The evidence adduced is on the whole strongly in support of the opinion that professional singers existed among the Anglo-Saxons as well as among other Germanic tribes of the sixth, seventh and ninth centuries.   The Anglo-Saxons seem to have been distinguished among the other Germanic races for their love of poetry and music, and the scop's art seems to have attained among them its highest development.   The scop flourished at a time when society was comparatively undifferentiated.   Hence his duties and his rank were not so clearly marked off from those of the other members of the primitive court as would have been the case among a more highly civilized people.   The scop is referred to again and again as a warrior, and, no doubt, was one.   The various aspects of the professional life of the scop and the variety of ways in which he was enabled to exercise an influence upon the society of his time have been sketched somewhat in detail. It has been shown that he was esteemed by his contemporaries, not simply as the poet but also as the sage, the teacher, the historian of his time. His power of moulding public opinion secured for him marked consideration from the great and powerful.